T0146849

Emotional Verse

ROBERT WEINHOFER

authorHOUSE®

AuthorHouse™
1663 Liberty Drive
Bloomington, IN 47403
www.authorhouse.com
Phone: 1 (800) 839-8640

Published by AuthorHouse   09/25/2015

ISBN: 978-1-5049-4885-2 (sc)
ISBN: 978-1-5049-4879-1 (e)

Library of Congress Control Number: 2015915126

Print information available on the last page.

Any people depicted in stock imagery provided by Thinkstock are models,
and such images are being used for illustrative purposes only.
Certain stock imagery © Thinkstock.

This book is printed on acid-free paper.

Contents

Dedication

This book is dedicated to my wife Linda, whose love and patience has guided me through the process of writing and having this book published. I would also like to thank the "Boy's Club" of my church for their support and inspiration, as they listened to recitals of my poems.

I would also like to thank Joe and Jen for granting me permission to allow the photo of their newborn twins, Joey and Aya, to be on the cover of my book. There is no stronger emotion on earth than when parents witness the birth of their children in all their pure innocence.

1

LOVE AND ROMANCE

Bliss

Under a lazy setting sun I lay me down to rest;
The fragrance of wild flowers permeates the air on a cool spring breeze,
Thoughts of my beloved are rekindled within the inner sanctum of my breast;
Wherever I am, the love of my life is always with me.

Memories of passion's kiss
Stir emotions in the corners of my mind.
On the wings of angels I am swept away into a realm of bliss,
The beautiful woman in my life so divine.

The wonders of love reach lofty heights,
What comforts abound when I dream of my lady love?
A mere mortal gliding on the jet streams of love's pure light,
Casting off the mundane mists of life as I rise above.

Father's Love

—∽—

His numerous titles have been inscribed on the scrolls
of life: Father, Papa, Pop, Daddy and Dad.
Whatever the title a loving Father always has a gentle smile
when we laugh and comforts us when we are sad.
He can be a disciplinarian when needed, but never rules with an iron fist.
An open-minded Father humbly apologizes when he is wrong;
his unwelcomed words or actions vanish in the mist.

A loving, thoughtful Father is a child's idol throughout their life-long days.
His endearing love is the lamp of wisdom that guides his
child through the darkness of troubled ways.
He is the pillar of understanding during the teenage "I know everything years."
And a Father's confidence in his child is as sturdy as a rock,
upon which his child leans when he confronts his fears.

And when on the waves of turmoil and indecision, his child is tossed about.
A vigilant Father is always there to rescue him from the stormy seas of doubt.
From his bank of common sense he has bequeathed
upon his child a wellspring of knowledge.
He is patient during outbursts of childlike stubbornness, and
an avid listener to his child's plans for the future.

And when we are lost in the jungle of life, we look to
our Father; he is our trusted pathfinder.
During the emotional rollercoaster of living, for our welfare
and happiness he is our stalwart defender.
There are times, however, when a Father's love for
his child cannot make the hurt go away,
It is in those trying moments of a health crisis, a loving
Father is there to console his child through the pain.

It is a worried Father who paces the floor for his stay
out late: "I forgot what time it was" child.
His child will never forget the disappointed look etched upon
his face when he says "All you had to do was call."
A loving Father is never perfect as he tries to support everything we do.
At the end of the day a tired Father wears that gentle smile when
he hears those four magical words "Daddy, I love you."

Father and Son

—⟋⟍⟋—

As a child you always found the time to play fun games with me.
Whenever I was afraid you held me close and my fears melted away.
You always read to me, "Twas the night before Christmas," my favorite story.
In time I knew the words by heart, you just smiled with glory.

When I was a teen I boasted how a great baseball player I was going to be.
You were there for me when my ego was crushed because I didn't make the team.
As a teenager, I rebelled against authority.
Through those growing pains your love and understanding
instilled in me the worth of responsibility.

You listened intently whenever I spoke of youthful
ambitions, which constantly in my heart burned.
You encouraged me to stand tall when faced with adversity,
and to be mindful of the value of a lesson learned.
Throughout my life you taught me that more in some things is not always best
And that failure is sometimes necessary on the road to success.

You were always proud of the challenges I have overcome;
Because of you I am the person I have become.
A father I am now with a wonderful wife and son
Walking in your footsteps, my life has just begun.

Mother's Love

—⁊⁊—

From a mother's womb the miracle of birth causes Heaven's Angels to smile.
And the innocence and frailty of human life can be found
in the arms of a mother nursing her newborn child.
There is an inherent worthiness in Motherhood as
she begins a life of new responsibilities.
And with each passing day a loving mother selflessly
tends to the welfare of her family.

Of a thousand wonders none is more magnificent than a mother's love.
She is the fire of hope, and the warmth of her love is
kindled within her gentle nurturing soul.
She wears the crown of a tireless multitasker from
dawn until long after the setting sun;
And we are constantly enthralled with a mother's
tenacity to complete the work she has begun.

A mother's love has a radiant glow like that of a rising sun;
And it is the well of love from which her undying
devotion is drawn for her precious little one.
Her outpouring of pride for her beautiful child
through feast or famine will forever endure.
Under a mother's watchful eyes childhood fears will remain obscure.

And during the growing pains of life, a concerned
mother will teach her child to stand tall.
She will be a safety net should her child stumble and fall.
If sorrow engulfs her child's life, a compassionate mother
will always be there to offer a tender "I love you."
And through the tests of time her child will learn that life
isn't always fair and that the sky isn't always blue.

But through the good times and the hardships, a loving
mother will reach out and render a soothing touch.
The years go by so quickly and from the depths of her
caring heart, those years she will cherish so much.
She gives her child wings to fly, but it is painstakingly
clear that she dreads goodbyes.
It seems that it wasn't so long ago when she cradled this
Heavenly gift in her arms and sang soft lullabies.

Love

—m—

The poet writes of love in verse and rhyme
Philosophers speak of love in terms of reason without fear or compromise
Through forgiving eyes, true love will stand the test of time.
Love is an unblemished painting of a beautiful flower, which never wilts or dies.

Love has a constant companion and its name is compassion
Love is sympathetic when life is cruel
Love holds dear the embrace of passion
Love champion's kindness and never wears the crown of a fool.

Love never seeks revenge nor does it abuse with an evil tongue
Love never feasts at the banquet of hate.
Love never blossoms in a heart of stone
And true love is never governed by chance or fate.

Love feels the pain and hurt of a misguided word
Love cries out in the night when trust is broken
Love can never mend when guilt is stirred
In the bosom of a deceitful heart, true love is never spoken.

The fabric of love is woven with delicate care
It is joined together with a giving bond
It reaches the majestic heights of heaven and never touches the lows of despair
To find true love is the greatest wealth ever found.

Passion

—∽—

Tempt these lips with an endearing kiss of pleasure
Bestow upon this wanting body a wellspring of untamed desire
And these timeless moments forever treasure
As passion's kiss fuels my sensuous fire.

Ecstasy, love's most narcotic gift,
Consumes my entire being with a warm loving glow
On an island of romance set adrift
As the tides of love ebb and flow.

And the embers of love are an eternal flame deep
within the ocean depths of my soul;
The fragrance of your seductive scent ignites a burning passion within me.
Your tender embrace of love sends my heart beating out of control
With every breath that I breathe; you are the love of my life for all eternity.

The Essence of Love

—∞—

An elderly man and an elderly woman walking hand in hand;
Two weary travelers on the road of life.
Many years have passed since their first walk together.
Their gait is much slower because of the ravages of Father Time,
But today is special and their hearts are filled with joy:
They are going to their favorite park for a picnic lunch
to celebrate their 55th wedding anniversary.
It will be a wonderful day because she is by his side.

They will laugh about stories from the past that no one else would understand.
He will tell her how happy and proud he is because she is his wife.
They will talk about the kids and grandkids and the joy they
have given them, and how they pray it could last forever.
They will reminisce about the good times and all
the promises he made to never whine.
They will look at pictures of her as a beautiful young
girl and of him as an innocent small boy.
How amazing it is to scroll through the pages of one's history;
The years have gone by so fast and he knows that he won't reach 85.

The old man is dying; they have both dreaded the day
when their little world would change forever.
She holds his hand as they relax in the calm of a summer sunset
His eyes swell up with tears of happiness
He remembers how they loved to go out dancing
and the first time she said, "I love you."
What will happen to her when he is gone is always on his mind?
Will the Almighty be kind to her at the end of her life?
Has he done everything to earn her respect and love?

If only he had more time to spend with her
He is but a shell of the man he once was, but because of her
devoted love he will depart this life with no regrets.
She knows that his time is short and her heart grieves with sadness
She leans over, kisses him on the cheek and softly whispers "I love you."
Her happiness has brought him so much joy and to leave her is so unkind.
Life is sometimes littered with potholes of grief and strife
But at the end of life's well-traveled road, isn't it amazing
to enjoy it with an Angel of compassion and love?

Tender Love

—◠◡◠—

The greatest gift in life is not found in the abundance
of wealth of a mighty kingdom.
It is the irreplaceable gift of time shared with loved ones near and dear to you.
And it is the growth of one's precious family, which is
cultivated and nourished from the soil of wisdom.
It is the warmth of a family's love that is soothing
like the soft beads of the morning dew.

And walking with our children and grandchildren in the
sunlight of their youth is a wonderful time spent.
What a blessing to listen intently to their ambitions as
we try to answer their countless questions.
Time passes so quickly and the joy and pleasantries
of those walks together are less frequent.
But our loved ones will always be with us as we gaze
into the pristine waters of life's reflections.

Strong family ties, are they not what makes life worth living?
Is it not one of life's master plans to be a part of
our loved ones growth and maturity?
Do we not bask in the sunshine of a life that is forever giving?
And a loving family, is it not the foundation for
happiness that lasts for all eternity?

2

SPIRITUAL

Faith Challenged

—w—

Under penalty of death Islamic terrorists torture me
to renounce my faith; I have chosen to die.
I am a Christian, my faith in Jesus Christ, my Savior, I will never deny.
I cannot submit to a religion founded on hate,
destruction, brute force, and coercion.
My free will is God-given; and I choose the religion of
my Savior, who taught love and compassion.

Because of my defiance, I am forced to kneel upon the ground.
My hands and feet are bound.
Soon the hooded executioner will draw his sword and end my life.
I pray Lord Jesus there will come a time when I will be
reunited with my children and my lovely wife.

In a terrorist world, destitute of pity, I beseech humanity to
reach the high point of the arc of moral reasoning.
My sadistic tormentors will end my life, but they will
be held accountable on the day of reckoning.
The dreaded messenger of death will take me to the
grave, but I will see a heavenly sunrise.
For I soon will walk with my Savior in paradise.

My Love for Jesus

—∞—

I have reached the summit of my troubled years,
I am the lamb lost in the wilderness; but because of Jesus'
love I can face all my tomorrows without any fears.
And in my heart and in my soul the fires of love for my Savior burn endlessly.
Although at times I may become mired in the quicksand
of doubt, my faith in Jesus will set me free.

I have never proclaimed to beat the drums of righteousness.
And my life, I sincerely profess, has not been lived under the dome of Godliness.
But when the final curtain is drawn and the last trumpets sound,
In the Kingdom of my Savior, I pray I will be found.

Although I am here for a brief sojourn, my time to
be received in Heaven is not yet at hand.
But before my demise, against racism, hatred, and
injustice I will serve my fellow man.
And I will not be a servant in the name of fame or high esteem.
I will serve to honor my Savior who died on the cross for me.

To free humanity from the heavy burden of sin He
gave His all on that cross of pain and agony.
Because of His sacrifice I will resist the evil temptations in my life courageously.
My Lord is my strength and refuge should I find myself wandering aimlessly.
With the power of His love I will endeavor to live out my life sinlessly.

Jesus forfeited His life so that death would not imprison me in eternal captivity.
He paid the ultimate ransom so that this wretched
soul could walk in the garden of eternity.
On that final judgement day when my physical body withers and dies,
In the serenity of Heaven, my spiritual body will live forever in paradise.

The Christian Journey

—∞—

On our Christian journey through life, our actions
can have an impact on many lives.
To walk in the footsteps of our Savior; to serve humanity should be our goal.
And while on our journey never judge the people
you meet along the way with cynical eyes.
Always believe in the life that you are living for
Jesus with all your heart and soul.

And as the uncertainties of life unfold, the gift of wisdom can be a precious jewel.
Never let your journey become overwhelmed with fiery impulses.
Always try to defend the goodness in life but never
argue with the rantings of a fool.
And never become a servant to life's excessive pleasures and indulgences.

There are many important qualities we need to
possess as we travel on our journey:
Love, charity, kindness and humility to name a few,
These helpful tools are necessary as we do our best to serve humanity.
Our journey can be spectacular as long as our faith in
Jesus and our fellow man is constantly renewed.

Sometimes our faith can be challenged by the
sadistic cruelty of the dregs of humanity,
Remain steadfast in the Christian faith, which was
bestowed upon us by our Savior and Redeemer.
Be ever mindful of the twists and turns of life which can lead us astray.
As the prince of darkness is always looking for a crack
in our armor of faith; he is a cunning deceiver.

Sadly, many will think of their journey as being a player in a traveling band.
For self-satisfying thrills they will wander the highways
and byways of life without direction.
Like so many misguided souls they will never reach the Promised Land.
They will never rejoice in Heaven with our Savior
who sacrificed His life for our salvation.

The End

—⧓—

Look into the face of a dying person, what do you see?
Do you see the face of a man burdened with the
wrinkled lines of age, pain or agony?
Or do you see the face of a man who has lived a full life without regret?
Prepared to meet his Maker, at peace with himself
in the tranquility of his last sunset.

As I travel down the stream of life for the last
time, what will onlookers see in me?
I pray they see a man who tried his best to serve humanity.
My heart and soul will not be saddened as I
envision my life without a tomorrow.
For I am going home to my Creator and He will cast away all my sorrow.

Family and friends, do not mourn for me
But comfort me with your prayers as I near the end of my life's journey.
And rejoice with me for soon I will walk through Heaven's gate.
Your love and kindness will be my passport into a Kingdom without hate.

When I finally enter into the deepest valley of mystery
I will not be afraid because Jesus, my Savior, will
guide me into His realm of eternity.
The sum of all my yesterdays will be laid to rest at Heaven's door.
And the icy hand of death will touch me no more.

The Last Goodbye

———

Soon I will witness the sunset in my life for the last time.
I can hear my Savior's angels calling me home,
What a glorious day it will be when I walk in
Heaven with Jesus who is so divine.
The joy, laughter, tears and sorrows of my earthly life will soon be gone.

In my family garden of life, the seeds of love I have carefully sown.
Death cannot hinder the growth of that love even
as the Grim Reaper knocks on my door.
But, my demise, I pray, will not cause my loved ones a woeful frown.
To my Savior I beseech cast away their sorrow; this I sincerely implore.

When I finally meet my maker will my death be calm and peaceful?
Will my last breath be silent as a whisper in the night?
No matter what the hour of my passing, I will rejoice
with my Redeemer who is all merciful.
The darkness of death cannot block out His love's pure light.

3
EMOTIONAL

Honor

—∿—

In every war humanity pays a terrible cost.
Generations of young men are forever lost.
There is no true glory in war only the senseless slaughter.
As the sacrificial lambs of innocence on the scorched battlefields lie scattered

We, the living, cannot comprehend the horrors of
war and its unprecedented carnage.
Nor can we begin to imagine the anguish of grief as
young men exhaust their last ounce of courage.
The stench of death is a solemn testimony to the brave soldiers
who gave their all for duty, honor, and country.
The laughter, dreams and ambitions of youth snuffed
out by the cruel weapons of unleashed fury.

I pray Lord Jesus give us the strength to extinguish forever
the flames of war and its unthinkable brutality.
Let us never need to erect white crosses on sacred ground;
but let us plant the seeds of life in the soil of morality.
And dear Jesus remove the pain and agony from wars ugly scar.
And let there come a time when future generations
of the young will ask, "What was War?"

Lost

—m—

There is a place filled with an endless gloom of misery
Where the souls of insanity dwell.
It is dark and cold and empty of mercy,
And a human body lives and breathes in the confines of this unspeakable hell.

It is a place where time strikes the hour with a heavy blow,
And where imaginary voices offer no relief from the madness of the mind;
It is a zombie state of unthinkable sadness, where tears of love will never flow
And where reality remains an eerie, shifting shadow of time.

How great a tragedy to be lost in the caverns of one's mind
Without a lifeline of happiness or joy;
Cast into the abyss of mental decline,
Forever imprisoned within the ghoulish walls of insanity, this poor wretched soul.

Stolen

—◆◆◆—

Looking into a mirror, there is a stranger's face staring back at me.
Who am I? Where am I? This is the unforgiving desert
of hardship known as Alzheimer's disease.
How dreadful life can be to exist solely on the blank pages of one's mind.
To be disoriented in the cruel wilderness of helpless
confusion, awaiting the passage of time.

As the past, present, and future identity of a person is stolen without a trace,
An unfortunate soul is lost in the darkness of a
deteriorating mind without hope of escape.
As Alzheimer's affliction progresses, the memory of loved
ones vanishes in the perpetual fog of forgetfulness.
Caregivers are devastated by the physical and
emotional strain as they toil in hopelessness.

It is beyond overwhelming the suffering these "Angels of Mercy"
endure as a precious life they care for slips away.
What a heartbreaking end to a life that has no recall of
yesterday and is destined for an ill-fated today.
Alzheimer's, the severest and most crippling storm of life,
never discriminates with the minds it ravages.
A distraught family prays for compassion as a loved one is
decimated by the harshest of intellectual damages.

Sadly, the dignity of the human person disappears into the mists of eternity.
To die without knowing who you are or who your loved
ones are is one of life's most tragic ironies.
But peace and closure may be found in loving memories we so dearly cherish.
I pray dear Lord that in our lifetime, the Gates of Mercy
open, and that Alzheimer's will soon be vanquished.

The Lost Causes

—∽—

What are lost causes? Are they not the causes we should fight for the most?
Is it not the basic principle of human kindness to
make every effort to right what is wrong?
If we see a man, woman or child begging for food in the
oppressive heat of summer or extreme cold of winter
Is it not our moral obligation to do what we can to
offer relief for their impoverished situation?
Are we not disappointed in prima donna athletes and flamboyant
rock stars who squander outrageous sums of money?
While hunger, disease and poverty rob so many of the simple pleasures of life
The irony of life in our country is that we have such an abundance of food.
Yet so many go hungry or even in the worst case
scenario, starve to death every day.

When we speak of lost causes none is more evident than World Peace.
World Peace is the most important lost cause we
should fight for with every fiber of our being.
Many wars have been fought and many are still raging on.
The horrific outcome of war is that untold lives are lost,
and that valuable natural resources are depleted.
Trillions of dollars are spent to feed the war machines around the world.
The amount of oil used in these wars alone could have added
a couple hundred years to the world's fuel supply.
Imagine if the money spent on war were used to
alleviate poverty, eliminate world hunger, and
Eradicate diseases such as: Cancer, Heart Disease, Diabetes and Alzheimer's.
What a wonderful world this would be!

I do not proclaim to have all the answers to save humanity from all its ills.
Nor do I profess to be a supreme intellectual.
What I am is a Christian who believes in what our Savior taught.
Serve your fellow man with love and compassion rather
than slaughter them with bombs, guns and bullets.
Mankind is moving closer to the most frightening
apocalypse of human history: Nuclear Holocaust.
The tragic reality of this unthinkable war is that the
victors and the vanquished will not survive.
Planet Earth as we know it will cease to exist.
We must pay heed to lost causes to prevent such a
catastrophe the world has never seen.
Let us work diligently to save humanity and to provide
a better life for our children and grandchildren.

The Soldier

—∞—

On a craggy mountaintop in a faraway land
Stands a lonely soldier with a rifle in his hand.
He is only nineteen this young Marine
To get home in one piece is his nightly dream.

He left the family he loves to fight on foreign soil;
The crackle of gunfire, his rifle recoils.
The bullet with no name silences the useless chatter;
The ghosts of fallen comrades in this desolate land lie scattered.

Back home the folks call him Billy Joe,
Alone on the mountaintop, it's hard to tell friend from foe.
His enemy is cruel and goes by the name Taliban;
To win the battle his unit must press on.

He will sleep on frozen ground under a blanket of snow.
Will he return home, he doesn't know?
With weapons of brutality the enemy in ambush lie in waiting,
The human toll is never abating.

As the battle rages on, the lives of so many are squandered.
Will there be an end to the madness, a young man ponders?
As screams of the dying chills the night.
A young Marine digs in to fight

He is proud to be a Marine and for his country he may die
Combat is brutal but to his mother he will lie
I'll be home for Christmas and have plenty of presents under the tree
Tell everyone I love them and kiss them for me

The young Marine is coming home but in a flag-draped coffin it will be
Taps are playing as the family gathers at Arlington Cemetery
He has paid the ultimate cost for his beloved country
The wellspring of youth is just a memory

4

MAN'S EVIL NATURE

The Downfall of Humanity

—ɷ—

I look to the Heavens in awe of its wondrous majesty
And suddenly my gaze becomes clouded with visions of human tragedy.
Humanity's hopes and dreams, I fear, are strewn on the horizons of insanity.
Hate, ideology, greed, and lust for power fuel the fires of absolute misery.

Barbaric atrocities silence the voices of reason.
The universal right to live free smolders in the ashes branded as treason.
An evil darkness blankets the whole of humanity.
In the killing fields around the world, the merciless bloodletting a bleak reality.

In a world consumed with hate, we must use our
investigative spades to uncover the soil of kindness.
We must ignite a fire of compassion in the dark souls of
those wretched followers of unthinkable madness.
And let us pray for deliverance for those who are
oppressed because of their Christian belief.
Please answer our prayers Dear Lord and put an end
to the unbearable suffering and untold grief.

Imagine

—⟋⟍—

Imagine an unwanted child bereft of life's simple necessities,
Her hopes and dreams thrown out with the evening garbage;
Imagine a bewildered child living within the
decrepit walls of despair and misery,
Vulnerable and afraid, her frail body trembling with visions of a dismal future.

Imagine an innocent child, her youthful spirit
crushed by the weight of her sorrow,
Her tormented life beset with nightmares that seem to last an eternity.
The one constant reality in her bleak life is a hopeless tomorrow.
Imagine a child living in this hostile, unforgiving climate of emotional instability.

Imagine a lonely abused child floundering in an ocean of doubt.
A frightened discarded human being teetering on the precipice of suicide,
Self-esteem lost in the mental corridors of her confused thought,
Her pitiful cries for deliverance from her oppressor's fall silent in the night.

To live without being loved, a grim existence in the life of a mistreated child;
The laughter and promise of youth stolen by ruthless, sadistic, dregs of life.
It is the dilemma of the ages when the human beast runs wild
And that a child of misfortune for a morsel of food begs nightly to survive.

The Religion of Evil

———

On the altar of terrorism the blood-stained cloth of humanity lies.
A lifetime of hatred and violence in the name of religion glorified,
Strapped with explosives, the flower of Muslim Youth dies.
Under the banner of fanatical Jihad the senseless loss of life is justified.

What evil mindset controls these messengers of mass murder?
To commit unthinkable carnage defiles the sacred laws of the human soul.
The Kingdom of Conscience is left barren in the
aftermath of the horrific slaughter.
The terrorist cares not for the loss of life; unimaginable
vengeance is their unified goal.

The death squads of terror are a blot on the pages of reason
as humanity begs for an end to the bloodshed;
But the merciless killings never cease, as young terrorists
are indoctrinated into a religion of suicidal hatred.
In their bloodlust crusade, innocent women and
children are counted among the dead.
To the morally bankrupt terrorist, a human life is not deemed sacred.

All faith based religions are rooted in the human
desires for love and compassion.
But the religion of the barbaric, unfeeling thugs of terrorism
revels in the hideous screams of the dying.
And the creed of these disciples of heinous crimes against
humanity burns in the all-consuming flames of coercion;
To kill any human being in the name of Allah is the religion
of a blunt instrument of unscrupulous brutality.

When will the Nations of the World employ zero tolerance to this evil menace?
When will compassion and reasoning answer the maddening cries for freedom?
As terrorism, its legions of death and psychotic
ideology draw nearer to hells furnace.
The religions of non-violent faith, armed with a dutiful conscience will
continue the crusade against the demon hordes of martyrdom.

Under Evil's Yoke

—∞—

Many will seek nourishment from the table of compassion.
Alas! Many will starve because of their race, color or creed.
Hungry for deliverance an enslaved multitude
will beg for the crumbs of salvation,
But they will be denied the simplest want or need.

Many will thirst for a cup of kindness
Their lives hanging in the balance as the cauldron of death is stirred.
But to the followers of gruesome mayhem; sympathy is a sign of weakness
And pleas for mercy from a frightened humanity will never be heard.

Mothers and Fathers will wander the bleak corridors of loneliness.
Numbed by grief, their only child lost in the fight for freedom.
The tragic loss of a son or daughter is an unbearable sadness.
Mourners will sob uncontrollably for their loved ones at the altar of martyrdom.

From the blood-soaked sands of human conquest
to the horrors of untold death camps,
The conscience of the morality of life is dust blowing in the wind.
Standing on the cliffs of oblivion, an eerie darkness covers our lands,
While the gatekeepers of hell revel at the sight of the evil souls of humankind.

5

HUMAN CONDUCT

Call to Freedom

—∿—

Mind numbing detonations from the cannons roar;
Unleashed mayhem knocks on Heaven's door.
Providence beams through the dark and dreary,
The colonial patriot so battle weary.

Watch fires of history burn through the night,
Shot and shell at morning's light.
Lost in brutal combat the "soul of human kindness"
The smell of death, a rude awakening to wars hallucinatory madness.

Hunger pangs are constant, while in the dead of
winter forlorn soldier's march in bare feet.
In the violent brutality of war, patriotism's destiny soon they will meet.
Bloodcurdling cries of revolution are at a frenzied high;
Charging into the firestorm of hell; many will not survive.

War's ugliness rears its Medusa's head as the innocence of youth is forever lost,
The paleness of death is the unthinkable cost.
From the depths of despair to hard fought victory
The Continental Army marches onward into history.

And when the siege guns fall silent and liberty reigns supreme
Immortal honor to the fallen that fought for their dream:
For these were the brave Sons of Liberty,
Their glorious cause echoes for all eternity.

America Lost

The home of the brave is burning and no one is left to put out the fire.
The welfare of the land of the free is dangling on
the threads of economic uncertainty.
What so proudly we hail is solemnly flying.
The barbarians are at the gates; America's doom they conspire.

Our Founding Fathers, their sacrifices and desire
Shook the world and raised the bar for humanity.
One nation under God her principles in the gutter are lying.
The soul of liberty is laid to rest on a funeral pyre.

Under Providence's watchful eyes, the voices of freedom rose higher and higher.
Our forefather's dream vanquished in the cesspool of profanity.
On the battlefields for freedom, sons and daughters are dying;
The youth of tomorrow navigate through the muck and mire.

American industry once the world did inspire,
Lack of imagination and a sense of pride have eroded our shores of opportunity.
Made in America is not worth buying!
As the doomsday clock counts down, the American dream will soon expire.

A Life Worth Living

—ᴡ—

I am at the crossroads of life's journey;
Many years have I misspent in my travels to nowhere.
Like a vagabond, I am but a blot on the pages of history,
The cupboard of generosity for my fellow man is sacrilegiously bare.

I have searched for, but never have I found, the "Holy Grail" of worthiness.
Will my life fade into oblivion at the lonely outpost of insecurity?
Can I overcome the pitfalls of my wretched ways
through simple acts of kindness?
Is there no greater endeavor in life than to serve humanity?

Will fate, the great trickster lure me into the murky waters of indecision?
These are the questions, which torment the sanctuary of my soul.
And through my trials, I have learned that wealth
cannot free a guilty conscience,
And that honor is more elusive than finding gold.

As I turn the pages of time, I have become a servant for humanity;
Hope for a better tomorrow lies in helping those who are less fortunate.
With guidance from my Savior, I have discovered a life worth living
Blessed with faith and compassion there is hope for a brighter future.

The Autumn of Youth

—m—

Autumn's brilliance fades with a stroke of our Maker's hand.
Football's gladiators ply their talents across the land;
Blood, sweat, and tears spent on a field of green 100 yards long.
The gods of coaching decide what is right and what is wrong.

The whispers of youth silenced in the turmoil of combative sport;
No mercy rabid fans exhort.
Yard by yard, through rain, sleet, and snow, high school warriors give their all.
But in the stadium of life yesterday's legends rise and fall.

Win, win and win the ultimate goal of unwavering courage.
All hail the conquering heroes, to the flower of youth pay homage!
Season complete and the autumn of youth is fast approaching.
And the turf wars are over and hard fought glory is already fleeting.

Coming of Age

—❦—

With our first breath a new life is just beginning.
When our eyes can see, they are open to a wonderful world of discovering.
From crawling on our knees to our first step, the early
years are a mixture of bumps and bruises.
Parents' guide us through the growing pains of our
youth with the language of becauses.

Loving parents try to set our moral compass in the right direction,
But even a happy child oft times becomes a servant of mindless objection.
The teen years drive our parents into a state of being hysterical;
That youth survives these tumultuous years is a miracle.

Off to college and our parents enjoy a sigh of relief,
But soon the empty nest shows telltale signs of grief.
The visits home our parents cherish;
Their child is maturing, gone are the days of being foolish.

A member of the work force, our lives have a new beginning.
We have begun plotting our future with a map of understanding
On the road of life we set forth with our eyes wide open;
Our challenges lie before us, and with confidence in
our ability we will meet them head on.

The Passage of Youth

The playgrounds of youth fade into yesteryear,
Echoes of laughter forever dear.
A young boy of eighteen with new worlds to explore,
The mazes of life ready to conquer.

Trekking through a wilderness of fears,
Bathed in confidence from every drop of blood, sweat, and tears.
A disciple of adventure and worldly thinking,
Charting his course for a life of discovering

Navigating courageously through the currents of life,
The hand of reason his steadfast guide.
Steering his way through the storms of pride,
Becoming a man, the days of youth gone by

Tossed about in the turbulent waves of life's voyage
Always trusting in the Almighty for safe passage
Overcoming the hardships of life, on bended knee to Him pay homage
Trusting in the Lord, youthful exuberance is blessed with unwavering courage.

The Rules of Life

—∿—

Someday and one day are words often spoken
One day I'm going to tell my wife how much I love her
Someday I will take my family on a well-deserved vacation
One day I'll visit a friend who is down on his luck
Someday I'll forgive those people who hurt me
One day I'll attend church
Someday I'll help a homeless person
One day I'll stop being a hypocrite and a bigot
Someday I'll find time to listen to my children
One day I'll find time to play with my children
Someday I'll be disappointed that the world doesn't revolve around me
One day I'll watch a romantic movie with my wife and not complain
Someday I'll discover that happiness can't be bought
Someday I'll do something for the betterment of humanity
One day I'll appreciate the little things in life
Someday I'll learn a valuable lesson; tomorrow is never a sure thing

6
NATURE

The Wonders of Life

—∿—

The explosive sounds of thunder, flashes of lightning, and wind swept storming
Billowy clouds, the vibrant colors of a rainbow across a blue sky
Moments in the sun, a breath of fresh air, a cool breeze on a hot summer's night
The priceless treasures of life money can't buy
All the senses bursting with delight.

Spring flowers, summer heat, and the magnificent leaves of an autumn's morning
The bitter cold of winter, white caps on the mountains high
Shadowy figures dancing in the moonlight
A blanket of snow under starlit skies
The living colors of the Northern Lights.

Nature awakens from a restful slumber to the melody of songbirds singing.
As we gaze at the radiant beauty of a majestic sunrise
Seasons of change a welcome sight
The landscapes of wonder, never to tame or compromise
The mysterious gloom of night disappears in the warm glow of sunlight.

Printed in the United States
By Bookmasters